CUSHIONS
AND
COVERS

CUSHIONS
AND COVERS

· · · · · · · · · · · · · · · · · · · ·

A PRACTICAL GUIDE TO CUSHIONS, THROWS AND COVERS FOR YOUR HOME

HEATHER LUKE

MEREHURST

First published in 1995 by Merehurst Limited,
Ferry House, 51-57 Lacy Road, Putney, London SW15 1PR

Copyright © Merehurst Limited 1995

ISBN 1 85391 477 0

A catalogue record of this book is available from
the British Library

Edited by Dulcie Andrews
Designed by Ivor Claydon
Special photography by Paul Ryder
Illustrated by Corinne and Ray Burrows

Typesetting by Cameron Typesetting
Colour separation by P & W Graphics, Singapore
Printed in Italy by Canale SpA

ACKNOWLEDGMENTS
The publisher would like to thank Sanderson for the use of the
photographs on pages 31 & 49; Osborne & Little for the photographs on
pages 7, 9 & 27; and Laura Ashley on pages 23 (right) & 53.
Photographs on page 12 by Paul Ryan, International Interiors; 14, 15
(top) & 45 by Lu Jeffery. Thanks also to the following companies who
lent their products and their time to the author and the stylist:
The Pier, Suzanne Ruggles, Belinda Coote Tapestries, Lunn Antiques,
Anna French Limited, Sussex House, The Rug Warehouse, The Futon
Company, Aero, Graham and Green, Crucial Trading, Colgone and Cotton,
Downers, Art in Iron, Baton Rouge, Kaffe Fassett and David Lewin Antiques.

Figures on all illustrations are marked in centimetres.

Contents

Introduction

Hand-made cushions are arguably one of the oldest types of soft furnishing. Small enough to sew by hand, at its very simplest, a cushion is no more than a piece of fabric holding an inner stuffing in place - with comfort as the primary function.

Man's first comfort requirement was 'somewhere to lay his head' and, in the past, mattresses were no more than large cushions made of strong cotton and filled with straw and ferns. Pillows were small bags filled with dried grasses and herbs, refreshed occasionally with flower water. Straw mattresses (palliases) have been slept on for centuries and may still sometimes be found in country areas. These certainly could not be described as luxurious, but were definitely more comfortable than wooden boards. Mattresses of wool and hair stitched in place were used by the more affluent. Cushions are now generally filled with cured feathers or fibre fillings. Fibre does not give such a good shape but is useful for those with an allergy to feathers.

Loose covers are a relatively new invention. In the past, all furniture was upholstered, with the top fabric firmly fixed to the chairs, sofas and headboards. In large country houses, a member of the household staff would be assigned to making slip covers in linen or cotton for all upholstered furniture to protect the expensive upholstery when rooms were not in use. These covers were usually made in simple white fabric which could be boiled and starched; they were made to fit very loosely and in no way resembled the fitted covers which we use today. Dining chair covers would often have the house owners' initials embroidered on the front of the seat backs. Hard-wearing upholstery fabric has always been the most expensive cloth to buy and, as upholstering is a skilled and labour-intensive job, having a piece of furniture upholstered is costly. Today, with our sophisticated laundering facilities, loose and throw-over covers offer a practical and economical addition or alternative to upholstered furniture; they can also be used to cover wooden furniture such as side tables, ottomans, and so on.

There are so many glorious fabrics available these days that, with a little skill and some direction, you can enjoy making attractive covers for all your furniture to give a fresh new look to your home. Cushion-making is simple, inexpensive and great fun. This book is packed with imaginative ideas to give you inspiration.

Heather Luke

Left: Black and white is always extremely chic and especially so when interesting patterns are combined.

Right: Checked fabrics make a strong design statement. Mix and match them (as shown here) for a clever 'country comes to town' look.

Section one
Colour and Style

Pillows and cushions are the most easily made of all soft furnishings but can also have a significant impact on a room. The use of different materials, textures and patterns, the infinite combinations of colours which can be chosen and the many details which can be added, make absolutely certain that nobody else will ever have the same furnishing combination and style that you have created for your interior.

Cushions can be carefully planned regarding size, shape, position, colour and texture to create an impact on their own, or two cushions might be designed to work together as a complete unit on a plain background. Alternatively, cushions may just happen - any number of cushions of different sizes and shapes, fabrics and trimmings, may be collected and thrown casually into a huge sofa or on to a large bed or window seat. There should be some thread of colour tone or fabric style for this to work - this will become instinctive as you get to know the colours which you most enjoy.

Neutral and all-white rooms may be designed to look traditional or contemporary - the style and colours of the accessories will set the tone. A single cushion in shocking pink will make a huge impact on an all-white room, whereas a cushion in a small print combining off-white and pale lilac will make very little impact but will add another dimension and lead the way for other mixed-colour fabrics.

Single-colour schemes can be most interesting to put together. Use textures and light and dark tones to give the variety which might

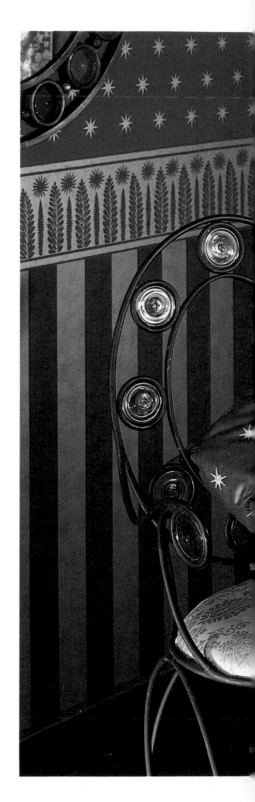

Cushions and covers can be as simple or as exotic as you like. Midnight blue and gold are a powerful combination for a formal dining room. The deep points on the table cover echo the star theme in the cushion fabric.

otherwise have come from pattern. A room full of cushions and covers in colours combining the pale brown of egg shells, yellows of clotted cream and the golden sparkle of sand will never be boring if you pay as much attention to the variety and texture of your components as Mother Nature does to hers. Find samples of matte linen, shot silk, crunchy-textured woven wool, fine cottons and self-patterned jacquards and pin them together to make a simple colour board. If you feel comfortable with this, choose which fabrics to use for cushions and which for covers. If you want to extend the palette further with soft pinks and apricots, or with strong reds and greens, find small pieces of coloured fabric, paint charts or magazine cuttings and add to the first colours to see just how much can be accomplished within a very small colour span. Colour choice will generally vary with each room, but the intensity and use of colours, textures and fabrics will have to be planned carefully for harmony.

Choosing colour schemes

It is easy to put together a scheme for a room; start with your room colour, add the tones and then the contrasts. Sofa and chair covers, cushions and other fabric accessories should be chosen together; think about the colours you would like to use in proportion to the amount that you will see in the room. When you have decided on the type of fabric and colour which you would like to use, ask your designer or retailer for large pieces so that you can drape them over your furniture and assess the effect in situ. Check that the colours will work as well by night as by day and then take the plunge. Measure carefully, estimate the quantity required and order.

You may decide all the sofas and chairs should be covered in the same fabric, with cushions adding other colours and interest; or each chair might be covered in a different colour. Two items covered in the same fabric give balance to a room, especially if there are a lot of odd chairs. Make sure that there are not too many legs showing; mix floor-length covers with shorter valances and wooden legs. Mix checked sofa covers with floral or small-print fabrics, or choose a range of varying sized checks, all in the same colour tones, for a sea of cushions on a floral sofa. Cover one sofa in deep pink with one chair in mid pink and

another in light coral, keeping the same hues. Cushion with patterned
fabric following the same colours, but add creams and whites in
woven patterns for relief.

Creating mood

Sometimes the same fabric can create quite different moods in
differing situations. Simple mattress ticking, piped and buttoned for
cushions in a Biedermeir chair, looks extremely elegant but, made
into scatter cushions and wrapped with a red or blue check, it
develops a distinctly country feel.

Seat cushions are generally made with a firm interior - just enough to
soften a hard surface and to give support but not enough to look
'fluffy'. Buttoning and piping in the deepest tone possible will give seat
cushions a smart structural identity, this more tailored look working
well with metal and wooden chairs and on window seats.

Less formal chair styles, such as wicker chairs and soft sofas, need
softer cushions. More feminine fabrics, lighter colours and self-toning
piping are sympathetic. Detailed ties and other embellishments work
well with less formal treatments.

Beds may be decorated in a number of different styles, relying almost
exclusively on the pillows and cushions. If you have no wish to change
all your bedding, simply make two bed pillows to add individual style.
Choose a plain back pillow and place another in front with some added
detail or striking print; or make two very large pillows and place them
face down one on top of the other. Use colours for impact - for
example, bright yellow ochre teamed with strong purple or blue.

The shapes and sizes of pillows are infinite: large round bolsters, huge
square pillows, frilled, bordered, tasselled and fringed, edged with old
lace, quilted, embroidered or plain, heart-shaped, rounded, oval and
tiny lace pot pourri pouches, will all combine happily with the
traditional shapes. Buy pieces of antique lace and stitch together, or
button the sides of an antique nightdress case to make a pillow;
mount patchwork or needlework on to linen and frill with organdie.

Comfortable bedheads can be made with thin box cushions fitted to a pole behind the bed or hung with ribbons tied to small coat hooks. Alternatively, make two large, bordered pillows, well stuffed, to prop up against a less than comfortable wooden or cane headboard.

Some fabrics which are not generally considered for soft furnishing are well worth considering for your schemes: unbleached linen, denim, artist's canvas, fine woven jute, gingham and even woven rugs and kelims. Explore any establishment which has fabric for sale and put your imagination to work. Denim slip covers are as hardwearing as jeans. Design and knit yourself decorative bed pillow covers, use leather off-cuts for piping, cut up sheets, napkins, glass cloths and even towels for cushions and covers.

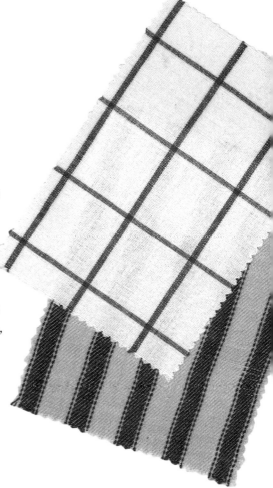

Trimmings in the form of cords, braid, tassels and fringes add an extra dimension and elegance to cushions and pillows. Look out for lovely antique trimmings with beads and toggles at flea markets, or use simple ric-rac or Tyrolean woven braid on country fabric.

Applied decoration in the form of stencilled designs and appliqué motifs can be used to make a plain fabric individual. Pick a motif from a fabric or wallpaper, or design a specific stencil. Cushions and throws, as well as fabric for fitted covers, can be decorated in this way.

From a practical point of view, it is always sensible to choose fabric that will stand up to wear and laundering. If you have a hectic life style, avoid any fabrics which might need a lot of attention to stay looking good. Find out as much as you can about your chosen fabric: will it fade in bright sunlight, is it machine washable, what is the wear-test strength? If possible, buy fabrics in natural fibres and wash the fabric before making up. Slip covers and seat cushions, in particular, should be suitable for laundering in a washing machine.

Cream fabric falls into full bunches on the smooth floor, creating a rich effect. The chair seats are covered in a matching cream. A cover like this completely changes the mood in the room.

Measuring and Estimating Fabric

The first step to making chair or sofa covers is to estimate how much fabric you will need. View your piece of furniture as a series of squares. Measure every area that you wish fabric to cover accurately. Each plane will have a widest point, which is the one to note down. Add 2cm (¾ in) for seam allowances to all measurements and 15cm (6 in) for tuck-ins on all seat pieces to determine the cutting sizes.

If you are using a fabric with a large pattern, either draw a diagram with the pattern repeat and any important elements to scale, so that you may place each piece exactly or, as a rule of thumb, add 20 percent extra to the basic quantity. Add 10 percent to the basic measurement for a small or all-over pattern repeat.

It is always best to make up your cover first using an inexpensive cotton fabric like calico, which has a firm weave, or an old sheet. Add an extra 6cm (2 ⅜ in) each way to the cut sizes to give yourself room for error. Pin each piece to the chair or sofa and, following the instructions, make up without the piping. Fit the cover and make any adjustments necessary before unpicking to use as the pattern for the main fabric. You will still need to fit the main fabric to the chair because another fabric will move and stretch in a different way to the calico but, having dealt with the seams and joins for the pattern, you will have so much more confidence with the real thing and avoid expensive mistakes.

Right: Piped and frilled cushions sit comfortably on a sofa with loose covers. It is also piped in a contrasting colour for extra design impact.

Below left: A combination of fabrics brings charm to this private setting. A plain cloth, covered by another edged with a contrasting plain tassel, covers an ordinary table. Note the chair has a frilled skirt in a completely different but complementary fabric.

Below right: Choosing one colour from the general pattern makes another strong statement as shown.

Cushion Pads

Cushion pads are available in all shapes and sizes: rectangular, round, square, boxed, heart shaped, oval and, if none of these suits, you can buy heavy-duty, feather-proof cambric to make your own. Rather than buy loose feathers, buy cushions and empty as many as you need into the new case. If you are fortunate enough to have old quilts filled with lovely soft eider down, use these. It is best to transfer the cushions outside, choosing a warm, still day. If you have to do the job inside, keep a vacuum cleaner handy to pick up the stray feathers.

Always buy the pad one size larger than your cover size to give a really plump cushion, as fillings always flatten with use.

The most usual fillings for scatter cushions are feather/ down and fibre. Curled poultry feathers are the least expensive and therefore the most widely used, but mixtures of feather and down give a softer, more comfortable cushion. Fibre fillings do not give such a good shape, but are useful for those who are allergic to feathers.

Seat cushions need to have high-quality fillings and, in this case, it is absolutely true that you get what you pay for. A seat cushion filled with poultry feathers will cost only one-tenth of the price of the same sized cushion filled with the finest down. Feather seat cushions always look comfortable and inviting but do not really have a smart enough appearance to

work with a contemporary sofa. If you like a sofa with a strong edge, choose a harder filling of either foam or foam and fibre mixed. In time, poultry feathers will uncurl and flatten and will not plump up at all: down feathers, however, are very fine and fluffy and puff up as soon as the cushion is 'plumped' and filled with air. It is therefore best to choose a mixed filling of down and feather and buy the highest percentage of down that you can afford. If your feathers have flattened, do not try to add more - this will be a false economy - simply replace them.

Large box seat cushions should have channels stitched across the width at approximately 15cm (6 in) intervals to keep the filling in place. This helps when plumping the cushion and prevents the filling from falling to the bottom of a back seat cushion. There is nothing worse than this!

Firm seat cushions are normally made from fire-retarding foam and covered with wadding. High-quality seat cushions have a central firm core bonded to softer outers, with the whole wrapped in wadding to give a firm seat with a softer look. You can make up your own using a central foam core with a mini feather quilt wrapped around; this seems to offer the best of both worlds - combining comfort and looks.

It is still possible to find upholsterers who will make hand-stitched horsehair cushions for traditional antique pieces and for the cushion enthusiast. Some small companies have recently started to make wool seat cushions which are firm, comfortable and durable.

It is always possible to order pads in special sizes from soft furnishing stores. Always check that the filling is the right one for your needs and that the pad will be made sufficiently large for your measurements. Check that large boxed cushions are channelled.

To keep feather cushions in good condition, plump them up every day. Drop each cushion on to the floor, one corner at a time, to force the filling into the corners and fill with air.

Choosing your Fabric

There is such an enormous variety of wonderful fabrics to choose from today, we only have room to provide a small selection here. The fabrics described below are generally for use in the main body of the cushion or cover; the more delicate, lightweight fabrics, such as lace or muslin, may of course be used to trim or overlay your cushion.

Natural Fabrics

SAILCLOTH
Stiff and hardwearing plain or basket weave made from 100 percent cotton or cotton/poly mix, this inexpensive material is generally used for deck chairs and tough outdoor purposes. Iron whilst damp as sailcloth creases easily.

HESSIAN
Coarsely woven from jute or jute and hemp, hessian is available in various weights and can be dyed in many colours. It is strong and hardwearing.

SEERSUCKER
A cotton fabric with vertical strips of alternating plain, tightly-woven cloth and loose-woven 'puckered' cloth in varying widths, seersucker is available in plain colours or stripes.

CALICO
Named after Calicut in India where it was first produced, calico is a coarse, plain-weave cotton in cream or white with 'natural' flecks. Available in many widths and weights, it is a relatively inexpensive fabric.

CAMBRIC
Made from linen or cotton, a closely-woven plain-weave fabric with a sheen on one side, cambric is used to make cushion pads as the close weave prevents feathers creeping through.

CANVAS
Often called cotton duck, this is a plain-weave cotton in various weights suitable for upholstered chair covers, slip covers and outdoor use. Canvas is available as unbleached, coarse cotton or more finely woven dyed in strong colours.

TICKING
Originally a fine striped woven linen used for covering feather mattresses, its characteristic tight, herringbone weave repelled feathers. Commonly in black and white, ticking is now woven in many colours and weights.

SILK NOILE
Light- to medium-weight silk in a natural colour, silk noile has small pieces of the cocoon woven in as flecks and is relatively inexpensive.

SILK SHANTUNG
Light- to medium-weight silk woven with irregular yarns giving a dull rough appearance, shantung is available in an extensive range of colours and gathers and frills well.

Heavy Plain Fabrics

CORDUROY
A strong cotton fabric woven to form vertical ribs by floating extra yarn across which is then cut to make the pile, corduroy should be pressed on a velvet pinboard whilst damp.

OTTOMAN
This is a heavy fabric woven to make horizontal ribs in cotton or cotton mixes. Extra weft cords are covered by the warp yarns.

VELVET
Originally 100 percent silk, velvet is now made from cotton and viscose. Care must be taken when sewing or the fabrics will 'walk'. Always buy a good quality velvet with a dense pile which will not pull out easily and always press on a pin board.

MOIRE
The characteristic 'watermarked' moiré is produced as plain-woven silk or acetate fabric progresses through hot, engraved cylinders crushing threads into different directions to form the pattern. This finish will disappear on contact with water.

FELT
The short wool fibres (staple) unsuitable for weaving are wetted, heated and put under pressure to form a flat, even, matted cloth. Fabric of varying rigidity is produced, depending on the type of wool used.

Woven Designs

DAMASK
This is a jacquard first woven in Damascus in silk, wool or cotton with satin floats on a warp satin background. Most damasks are self-coloured and can be made up reversed for a matte finish.

BROCADE
Brocade is traditionally woven using silk, cotton, wool or mixed fibres, on a jacquard loom, in a multi- or self-coloured floral design. Traditional motifs such as cherubs, vases, ribbons, bunches of flowers and so on are mixed together.
A true brocade has additional coloured weft threads which float on the back and are brought forwards on to the front to produce the pattern on the right side. Sometimes metal threads are used to give an extra dimension to the design.

CREWEL
A plain-woven, natural cotton background embroidered in chain stitch in plain cream wool or multi-coloured wools, crewel work used to be a popular hobby. It is now mostly hand-made in India in floral and Eastern designs.

TAPESTRY
A hand-woven fabric in many colours with a ribbed surface, tapestry traditionally depicted an historical scene. The term is now used to describe heavy, stiff fabrics woven in several layers to produce a hardwearing, multi-coloured result, used for heavy-duty upholstery and heavy curtains.

Woven Checks

TARTAN
Authentic tartans belong to individual Scottish clans and are woven or worsted fine twill weave with an elaborate checked design. Both warp and weft have threads with mixed colours. Tartan designs are now worked in cotton, and also in silk to produce elegant shimmering fabrics.

GINGHAM
A plain-weave fabric with equal width stripes of white plus one other colour in both warp and weft threads to produce blocks of checks or stripes, gingham is 100 percent cotton or a cotton mix.

PLAID
Wool or worsted cloth in square or rectangular checked designs, plaid is usually woven in two or three colours and often used for shawls or more tightly woven for sporting clothes. Use to upholster stools, fenders, chairs or sofas.

Printed Designs

CHINTZ
Traditionally a cotton fabric with Eastern designs using flowers and birds, chintz often had a resin finish which gave a characteristic sheen (glaze) which repels dirt. The term chintz is now mostly used to describe any patterned or plain glazed fabric. The glaze will eventually wash out, so dry-cleaning is recommended.

TOILE DE JOUY
Created in France in 1770, pastoral designs in one colour printed on to calico cloth (from India) using copper plate printing techniques, toiles mix very well with silks, muslin, light calico, checks and stripes

INDIENNES
Since the mid 17th Century one or two specialist French companies have been printing 'les Indiennes' by hand. Small colourful patterns are printed on to calico using carved blocks also imported from India and the traditional colours were all originally created using natural dyes. Today these designs are sometimes referred to as Provençal prints.

Section two

The Projects

Project 1:
•••••••••

Making Scatter Cushions

Scatter cushions can be extremely functional, for example when fitted in the small of the back in a hard or uncomfortable chair. A large soft cushion can be used as a pillow, or plumped up and arranged to make a comfortable headrest. The great advantage of scatter cushions is that they can be made of the finest material - the small quantity of fabric needed makes the luxury affordable.

Padded False Oxford Cushion

Our cushion has been made 33cm (13 ¼ in) square with a 9cm (3 ½ in) border.

Materials

- main fabric - front 54 x 54cm (21½ x 21½ in) - back 59 x 54cm (23½ x 21½ in)
- 4 oz polyester wadding - 2 squares 51 x 51cm (20 ⅜ x 20 ⅜ in)
- 30cm (12 in) zipper
- 35cm (14 in) square feather pad

1 Cut 14cm (5 ½ in) from the back (59cm [23 ½ in]) length. Pin the two pieces back together, preparing a 2cm (¾ in) seam into which the zip is to be inserted. Stitch 13cm (5 ¼ in) in from each side. Press. Insert the zip (see page 61).

2 Place the back piece on the worktable right sides down. Lay the two squares of wadding on top of each other and cut out 34cm (13 ½ in) from the centre. Place on the cushion back and tack in place. Turn over, open the zip 5cm (2 in) and pin the front to the back, right sides together. Stitch all around 1.5cm (⅝ in) from the edge. Trim corners.

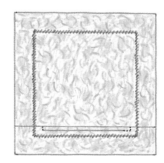

Open the zip fully and turn the cover to the right side. Use a point turner to make good square corners. Tack a line 9cm (3 ½ in) in from the outside edge. Satin stitch all around with contrasting thread. Remove tacking and press.

Envelope-style Cushion

Our cushion was made to fit a pad 40 x 30cm (16 x 12 in).

Materials

- fabric 1 - 73 x 46cm (29 ¼ x 18 ⅜ in)
- fabric 2 - 66 x 43cm (26 x 17 in)
- 40 x 30cm (16 x 12 in) feather pad
- 1 button

1 Fold fabric 2 in half lengthways and stitch 1.5 cm (⅝ in) seam on long side. Turn out and press. Lie fabric 1 flat, right side up and place this rectangle over centrally, 1.5cm (⅝ in) in from either side. Stitch the side seams as below.

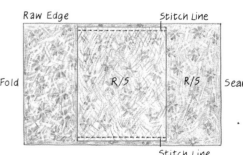

Padded False Oxford Cushion, Envelope-style Cushion, and Cushion with Tied Sides.

Project 1: *Making Scatter Cushions*
• • • • • • • • •

2 Fold fabric 1 in half lengthways, right sides together, and stitch the short sides together. Trim the point. Turn the cushion cover right side out and press. Fold under the raw edges and stitch close to the fold line. Either make a buttonhole on one of the flaps and stitch the button opposite or fill the pad and stitch a button through both layers.

Cushion with Tied Sides

Our cushion was made to fit a pad 45 x 35cm (18 x 14 in).

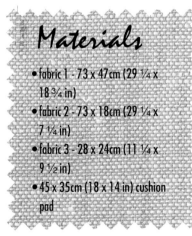

Materials

- fabric 1 - 73 x 47cm (29 ¼ x 18 ¾ in)
- fabric 2 - 73 x 18cm (29 ¼ x 7 ¼ in)
- fabric 3 - 28 x 24cm (11 ¼ x 9 ½ in)
- 45 x 35cm (18 x 14 in) cushion pad

1 Make the ties (see below) by cutting fabric 3 into four pieces 28 x 6cm (11 ¼ x 2 ⅜ in). Press in half lengthways and press each side in half again. Turn one end in 12mm (½ in). Stitch close to the edges.

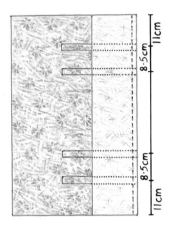

2 Place fabric 1 on a flat surface, right side up, and position the ties as shown. Pin fabric 2 over and stitch a 1.5cm (⅝ in) seam. Press seam. Fold in half lengthways and stitch around the two sides. Snip corners, turn right side out and press. Fold in 2cm (¾ in) double turning on fabric 2 and stitch. From the right side, press fabric 2 towards the inside and pin so that 1.5cm (⅝ in) is left showing. Machine stitch exactly where the two fabrics meet to hold the flap in place. Insert the pad behind the flap and tie the ties.

MAKING TIES

Tie a piece of seam binding tape or a strip of fabric in position to find out how long and how wide your ties should be when finished. Functional ties must be sewn into place securely during the making up of the cushion. A smart treatment might need short knots or a tie tied like a bow tie, whereas a feminine treatment might warrant long double bows. A rouleaux tie will give a softer finish than a folded tie will give.

MAKING A ROULEAU TIE

Cut a strip of fabric four times the width of your finished tie and 3cm (1 ¼ in) longer. Fold in half lengthwise, right sides inside, enclosing a piece of cord which is longer than the strip of fabric. Stitch along the short side to ensure it is securely in place. If the rouleau is quite wide, knot the cord as well. Stitch along the length, just away from the centre and towards the raw edges. Cut across the corner, pull the cord through, at the same time turning the fabric right side out. Cut the cord off, and the end of the fabric. Press the raw edge under and slipstitch with very small stitches to finish the tie.

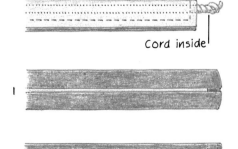

Cord inside

The fruits of a labour of love are displayed in this fabric and the cushion combination.

Lush velvet fabric edged with tasselled fringing make you want to hug these cushions. The plain colours are perfect with such a rich tapestry background.

A pretty combination of stripes, small florals and frills make this an enchanting corner to while away a sunny afternoon. The colour and pattern combination is light and breezy.

Project 2:
● ● ● ● ● ● ● ● ●

Using all the Trimmings

Tassels, rosettes, cut fringes, bullion fringes, long fringes, short fringes, cords, fan-topped edgings in linen, cotton and silk, olives in wood and jasmines in gold and silver - passementerie is available in as many colourful combinations, shapes and sizes as can be imagined. Trimmings add a luxurious, professional feel. Whether you are adding a simple cream cut fringe to plain cream cotton or an elaborate combination of ropes, tassels and fringes to a fabulous silk damask, the result is always to make the first fabric more elegant.

It is important to match the style of the trimming to the style of the cushion. Adding a lush trim to a plain and simple cotton fabric will not look correct. Always make sure the trim is of the correct Period if using a Period theme. For example, a Victorian-style fringe on an Art Deco style fabric will look odd.

Cushion with Tied Corners

Materials

- fabric 1 - 65 x 65cm (26 x 26 in)
- fabric 2 - 65 x 65cm (26 x 26 in)
- 3m (3 ½ yd) flanged cord or piping cord
- 45cm (18 in) square feather pad
- 35cm (14 in) zipper

1 Cut front and back as shown. The cushion part should be 48 x 48cm (19 ¼ x 19 ¼ in) and the 'ears' 12-15cm (4 ¾ - 6 in) long, 7cm (2 ¾ in) wide where they meet the cushion and 9cm (3 ½ in) wide at the widest part. Place right sides together and make notches.

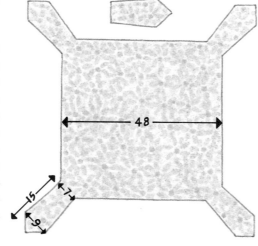

2 From the spare fabric cut eight 'ears' to the same size. Stitch each loose 'ear' to a fixed one, right sides together. Trim seams. With the front piece flat, right side up, pin piping or cord between each corner and tuck the ends inside. Stitch. Pin the two pieces together for 3cm (1 ¼ in) along the bottom edge and insert the zipper. Stitch back and front together, matching notches, leaving 5cm (2 in) openings at each corner. Turn right side out. Check to see that no stitching is visible. If there is, re-stitch closer to the piping. Turn each ear to the right side and press. Fold under the raw edges and slipstitch to neaten.

Tassels, bows and buttons add an extravagant feel to these three cushions.

Project 2: *Using all the Trimmings*
. . . .

Buttoned Stool Cushion

Measure your stool and make the cushion 10 percent larger to allow for 'shrinkage' when the buttons are stitched on. Our stool measured 36 x 30cm (14 ⅜ x 12 in).

Materials

• fabric - 2 pieces, each 43 x 37cm (17 ¼ x 14 ⅝ in)
• 1.6m (70 in) flanged cord
• 4 or 8 tassels
• 32 buttons
• buttonhole thread and a buttoning needle
• 40 x 35cm (16 x 14 in) feather pad

1 Place the two pieces of fabric right sides together and notch at least once along each side. Stitch the cord to the right side of the front piece. Pin the back to the front, right sides together, matching notches and stitch, leaving a 12cm (4¾ in) opening on one side.

2 Snip across corners and turn right side out. Insert the feather pad and slipstitch to close the opening. Plan the button positions on back and front. Using light upholstery string or buttonhole thread, stitch the buttons through the feather pad, opposite each other, pulling tightly.

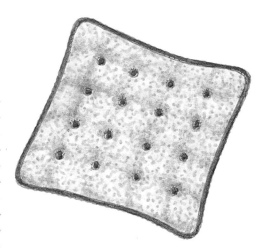

Button stool cushion showing placement of buttons.

Formal Bolster

Materials

• feather bolster-15cm (6 in) diameter x 46cm (18 ½ in)
• fabric 1 - 50 x 49cm (20 x 19 ¾ in)
• fabric 2 - 2 pieces, each 49 x 18cm (19 ¾ x 7 ¼ in)
• 1.1m (44 in) flanged cord
• 4 tassels
• 2 covered buttons, 2.5cm (1 in) diameter
• 1m (40 in) of 1mm (¹/₁₆ in) tape

1 Pin the flanged cord to the right side of both ends of fabric 1. Tuck ends inside 1.5cm (¾ in) from each edge. Stitch. Pin both pieces of fabric 2 along the cord stitching lines and stitch just inside these lines. Fold in half lengthways and stitch long side.

2 Make 1.5cm (⅜ in) turnings at each end, leaving 1.5cm (⅜ in) gap to thread tape through. Tighten the tape on one end and knot. Tuck the knot inside and cover with a button. Attach tassels. Insert the bolster pad and close up the other end.

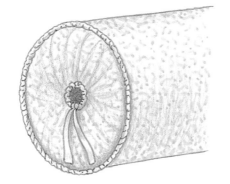

Tying the ends on a formal bolster.

Cotton checks in mixed colour combinations can be trimmed with cotton fringes, edgings, braids, buttons and tassels in blues, green and yellow.

Here is an interesting colour combination of brilliant aquamarine and rich red, both touched with imaginative gold button and gold cord trimmings. Such expressive use of passementerie is an example to follow in your own style.

Project 3:
• • • • • • • • • •

Making Boxed Cushions

Boxed cushions are one of the most useful soft furnishings to be able to make. Any seat cushion which is to provide long-term comfort needs depth, so the cover will need to be gusseted and the cushion 'boxed'. Wicker chairs, upholstered sofas, metal chairs and wood or cane armchairs all need to have seat and back cushions which are boxed. Almost any fabrics are suitable, obviously depending on the use to which the chair is put and your chosen colour scheme, but choose washable fabrics for outdoor or heavy-use chairs. Metal-framed chairs are structurally strong and look very good with a definite stripe; wicker chairs have a lighter feel and suit a softer stripe, floral chintz or country check.

Boxed Cushion
(Piping may be added as below for a sofa or chair seat cushion)

Materials

- feather or foam cushion pad - 65 x 45 x 10cm (26 x 18 x 4 in)
- fabric - 2 pieces 68 x 48cm (27 ¼ x 19 ¼ in) 1 piece 138 x 13cm (55 x 5 ¼ in) 2 pieces 88 x 9 cm (35 ¼ x 3 ½ in)
- 85cm (34 in) zipper

1 To set the zipper into the two pieces 88 x 9cm (35 ¼ x 3 ½ in), press under 2.5cm (1 in) on each of the long sides. Open up the zip and pin one side very close to the teeth. Stitch. Close the zip and place the fold over the teeth so that the first stitching line is not visible. Pin and stitch.

2 Join the short side of the other gusset piece to the closed zip end. Place the front and back pieces together and make notches along each side.

3 Starting with the open end of the gusset placed 10cm (4 in) from one back corner, pin the gusset to the front piece 1.5cm (⅝ in) from the raw edge. At each corner, stop 1.5cm (⅝ in) from the end and snip 1.5cm (⅝ in) into the gusset. Fold the fabric to make a right angle and continue pinning.

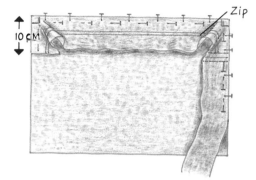

4 Pin the two gusset ends together. Unpin 10cm (4 in) and stitch together. Re-pin this 10cm (4 in) and stitch all around. Open up the zip 10cm (4 in), pin the gusset to the back piece in the same way, matching notches. Stitch. Turn right side out and press.

Neutrals, always smart combinations for furnishings, are shown here in upholstery-weight fabrics for sofa and chair cushions.

Project 3: *Making Boxed Cushions*

Piped and Buttoned Mattress

Our mattress measured 180 x 90cm (72 x 36 in).

Materials

- fabric - 2 pieces 183 x 93cm (74 x 37 ¼ in)
  1 piece (for gusset)
  543 x 18cm (18 ft l ¼ in x 7 ¼ in)
- 11m (3 ft 6 in) piping
- 56 buttons
- lightweight upholstery thread and buttoning needle

1 Place the two larger pieces of fabric right sides together and notch several times along each side. Pin piping all around the right sides of both pieces, 1.5cm (⅝ in) in. At corners, stop 1.5cm (⅝ in) before the end and cut right to the piping stitching line. Fold the piping at an angle of 90 degrees to make a really square corner. Join as shown on page 63. Stitch just outside the piping stitching line.

2 Pin the gusset to the piping line on one of the main pieces of fabric, starting at one corner and snipping right into each corner to keep square. Join the two gusset ends together on the corner.

3 Machine stitch as close to the piping as possible. Turn to the front and check to make sure that the first stitching line is not visible. If it is, re-stitch closer to the piping. With right sides together and matching notches, pin the

other side to the gusset along one long and two short sides of the second main piece of fabric. Stitch, double-stitching the open corners. Check your stitching as before. Turn right side out and press. Insert the mattress and slipstitch the gusset opening to the piping with lightweight upholstery thread.

4 Measure buttoning positions and mark with crossed pins: mark position on bottom and top of mattress. Stitch button in place on top and push the needle through to the underside to catch another button. Pull thread back through and pull taut.

The piped and buttoned mattress below measures 180 x 90cm (72 x 36 in). Place the first row of buttons 15cm (6 in) in from one long edge, then place the second button 30cm (12 in) across and the third button, 30cm (12 in) across, making it 15cm (6 in) from the far edge. Begin the second row of buttons 30cm (12 in) in from the edge. Place the second button 30cm (12 in) toward the far edge, as shown in the illustration. Continue along the mattress in this way.

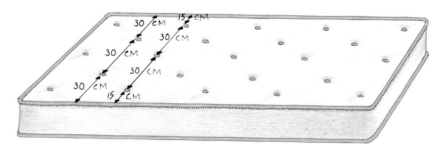

These striped and checked fabrics need to be a strong weave for this type of cushion.

Deep feather cushion pads with boxed covers in a traditional settle seat look comfortable and inviting. Yellow and green stripes dominate this country fabric and are perfectly matched through the gusset and on to the seat, whilst piping is used to add a crisp edge.

Project 4:

• • • • • • • • •

Making Throws

Throws are one of the most interesting and useful furnishing accessories to be re-discovered in the last few years. Lengths of fabric, bedcovers, quilts, blankets and rugs from all over the world giving infinite style choice and individuality to furnishing are now so readily accessible with the increase in travel possibilities and retail awareness. At one time, the only way to obtain a beautifully-coloured Aztec Indian rug to throw over your sofa was to visit South America. This is, of course, still the best way, but it is now possible to buy one in almost any other country.

Indian cotton bedcovers, from blue and white to lovely earthy reds and terracottas, Italian chenille weaves in deep rich colours, crewel-worked designs in cream on white, lengths of hand-printed cottons from Africa in fantastic colours and designs and Scottish tartan rugs can all be made into lovely throws and covers. Full-sized covers in many and varied Amish quilt designs are available as hand- and machine-made copies for beds and sofas, and as many books with patterns and advice to make your own. Use two or three throws folded back together on a bed, or two with complementary designs and colours on a large sofa - or make your own patchwork from remnants of fabrics to evoke happy memories.

Throw

Materials

- fabric 1 - 200 x 135cm (80 x 54 in)
- fabric 2 - 200 x 135cm (80 x 54 in)
- fabric 3 - 200 x 135cm (80 x 54 in)
- 270cm (3 yd) fringing

1 Place fabric 1 on to the worktable and mark diagonally from each corner into four triangles. Cut and repeat with fabric 2. For the front, place the two 135cm (54 in) triangles of fabric 1 at top and bottom on the worktable. Place the 200cm (80 in) triangles of fabric 2 on either side as illustrated.

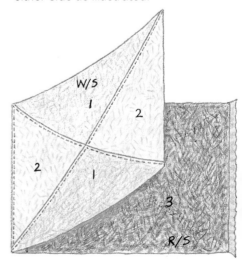

Strong colours and an interesting fringe make this throw into a work of art.

Project 4: *Making Throws*
· · · · · · · · · ·

2 Pin the top and right-hand triangles together and stitch. Pin the bottom and left-hand triangles together and stitch. Stitch these two large triangles together, matching the seams at the centre exactly. Use as many pins as necessary to prevent the fabric stretching on the cross.

3 Cut the fringe into two and pin to the front piece along both short ends. Stitch. Place this joined piece onto the worktable, right side up. Place fabric 3 (lining) over, right side down, matching corners. Stitch all around leaving 30cm (12 in) opening on one long side. Snip across corners, turn and slipstitch to close opening. Stitch a large button or tassel to the centre where the fabrics meet. Use the remaining pieces to make cushions following the ideas in Projects 1 and 2.

Fringe under

R/S

W/S

A luxurious look on a plain dark sofa is created with this bordered throw and contrasting cushions.

Richly coloured stripes complement the cushions providing a warm, vibrant effect.

Hand-stitched appliquéd naive animal shapes on an Indian red background lifts an otherwise plain neutral sofa.

Left: Choose a striped fabric with a co-ordinating check pattern for a chic effect.

Project 5:
• • • • • • • • • •

And so to Bed Pillows

Dressing the bed is a very personal matter, and perhaps the only area in the house which is really for you. Furnishings in the main rooms of any home are chosen according to your character but with others' needs and wishes very much in mind. Bedcovers and pillows offer excellent opportunity for individual design, colouring and detail. Strong colours and plain edgings can be used to great effect in a minimal bedroom, as can lovely floral designs with ribbon details and crisp white linen in a cottage-style room. Bed pillows usually consist of one or two for function and more for decoration. A bed piled high with lacy cushions may look wonderfully romantic but the practical will ask 'wherever do the cushions go at night?' Make sure you have a handy sofa or chair to hold them all.

Pillow with Border

Our pillow size was 75 x 50cm (30 x 20 in) but any size will do.

Materials
- 1 pillow, 75 x 50cm (30 x 20 in)
- fabric, 2 pieces, each 92 x 61cm (36 ¾ x 24 ¾ in)
- 60cm (24 in) zipper

1 Pin the front and back pieces right sides together and stitch along the bottom long edge for 31cm (12 ⅜ in) each side, using a 2cm (¾ in) seam allowance. Insert the zip as shown on page 61. Open the zip a few centimetres and pin the other three sides

together. Stitch, 1.5cm (⅝ in) in, trim corners and neaten seams. Turn right side out, make good sharp corners and press.

2 Mark a line 7cm (2 ¾ in) in from the top and sides. Tack securely. Satin stitch following the tack line. Remove tacking threads.

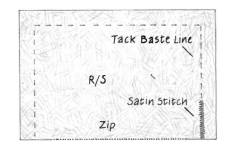

Pillow with Frilled Edge

Materials
- 1 pillow, 75 x 50cm (30 x 20 in)
- fabric - 2 pieces, each 80 x 53cm (32 x 21 ¼ in) for front and back
  - 1 piece, 53 x 22cm (21 ¼ x 8 ½ in) for pillow flap
  - 1 piece, 5m x 11cm (16 ft x 4 ⅜ in) for frill
- 12mm (½ in) matte ribbon, 5m (16 ft) long

1 Join the frill ends. Press 12mm (½ in) to the right side along the 5m (16 ft) length. Pin the ribbon to this, so that the folded edge of fabric is just under the ribbon and the raw edge is covered completely. Stitch in place at either side of the ribbon. Stitch a gathering thread 1.5cm (⅝ in) from the edge along the opposite side.

2 Mark the frill into four sections: two of 1.5m (62 in), and two of 1m (40 in). Each of these marks will be at one corner of the pillow. Pin frill on to the front, pleating gathers evenly along each side. Stitch in place.

Bold checks and stripes combine to create a stunning effect in a bedroom.

Project 5: *And so to Bed Pillows*

3 Make a 1.5cm (⅝ in) double turning along one long side of both the pillow flap and the back piece. Pin pillow flap to one side of the front, enclosing frill. Stitch inside the previous stitching line. Pin the back to the front and the pillow flap over. Stitch in place, turn right side out and press.

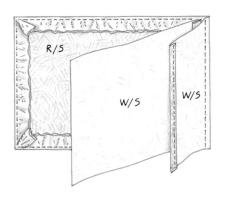

R/S
W/S   W/S

Pillow with Buttoned Border

Materials

- 1 pillow, 75 x 50cm (30 x 20 in)
- fabric 1 - 1 piece, 81 x 53cm (32 ½ x 21 ¼ in) for front
  - 1 piece, 58 x 53cm (23 ¼ x 21 ¼ in) for back
- fabric 2 - 53 x 43cm (21 ¼ x 13 ¼ in) for buttoned flap
- 5 buttons , approximately 3cm (1 ¼ in) diameter
- cotton stiffening, 5 x 2cm (¾ in) squares

1 Stitch pillow flap to back piece, right sides together. Fold flap in half and stitch from the fold towards the seam for 20cm (8 in), taking 1.5cm (⅝ in) seam allowance, top and bottom. Snip across the seam allowance at the end of the stitching line, neaten and fold right sides out. Fold the raw edge of the flap under and pin over the seam to enclose.

2 Make a 2cm (¾ in) double turning on one short side of the front piece. Pin the back to the front along the other three sides. Stitch, neaten seams and corners and turn right side out.

3 Make five buttonholes on the flap and position buttons on the pillow front to line up. Stitch a small piece of cotton stiffening under each button

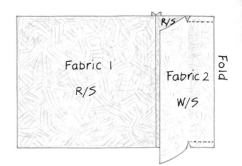

R/S
Fabric 1
R/S
Fabric 2
W/S
Fold

Rich satin oval-shaped cushions bring an Oriental theme into a bedroom. These have a thick piped cord edging.

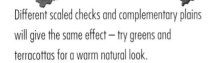

Different scaled checks and complementary plains will give the same effect – try greens and terracottas for a warm natural look.

White fancy cushions and green and white striped pillows combine here to create a fresh, summer mood.

Project 6:
• • • • • • • • •

Making Sofa and Chair Covers

A rmchairs and sofas, whether inherited or bought second-hand, often do not need extensive and expensive upholstery repair but will sometimes be covered in a fabric which is unsuited in style, colour (or both) to your taste. However, because seating furniture dominates the room, something has to be done.

Making a slip cover is not the easiest project to undertake for a beginner but, with a little basic knowledge, the capable amateur can tackle this with ease. Begin with box cushions and then make a simple slip cover in calico for a small bedroom or bathroom chair to increase your knowledge and, once you see how easily the pieces fall into place, you will soon become confident. Making slip covers can quickly become a passion; it is enormously rewarding to see an ugly piece of furniture turn into something lovely as you work.

Chair Cover

Measure your chair accurately to work out how much fabric you will need and the best way to cut out. View the chair as a series of squares.

inside back	A x B
outside back	C x D
inside arm	E1 x H
outside arm	E x F
seat	K x L
skirt (optional)	J + E2 + C2 (outside back measurement) + E2

Add 12cm (4 ¾ in) to the bottom of the inside arm and

the inside back measurement. This is for your 'tuck-in' - where the fabric will push down between the seat and back holding the seat piece in place. Add 2cm (¾ in) to all other measurements for seam allowance.

Decide where you would like to show the contrast piping and measure.

Materials

- fabric 1 as estimated (see above)
- fabric 2, made into piping as estimated (see above)
- tight-woven cotton to stiffen the skirt
- calico for pattern

1 Cut the cover in calico first to make a pattern. Cut out pieces as estimated. Over-cut the calico by approximately 5cm (2 in) each way.

2 Mark with a line of pins the centre back, seat and outside back on your chair. Finger-fold the two backs lengthways and line up the folds along these pinned lines. Without moving the fabric, pin the

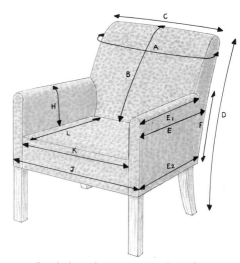

A scalloped edge makes an interesting change for a stylish chair valance. Cut the first scallop shape by drawing around a wine glass, tea cup or saucer and repeat the shape to fit across the width.

Project 6: *Making Sofa and Chair Covers*
• • • • • • • • • •

pieces lying against the chair to the chair. Gradually unfold the other side and pin to secure. Pin these two pieces together around the back, from just above the arms. Ease, pleat or dart the corners. Trim away to 2cm (¾ in) seam allowance and make notches to follow when stitching the seam.

3 Pin the inside and outside pieces of each arm together in the same way.

Pin each arm piece to the outside back from the bottom to the top of the arm (fig 1). Cutting around the arm is probably the most difficult part of a making a chair cover. The outside and inside arms should be joined together as near to the back as possible. Pin the inside back fabric out of the way and, working with the inside arm piece only, fold it back on to itself following the curve of the arm. You will need to snip this fabric close to the chair to make the fabric lie flat . When the fabric is quite flat, mark the shape of the arm clearly with a thick pencil. Trim away any excess fabric to 2cm (¾ in), remembering to keep the tuck-in allowance.

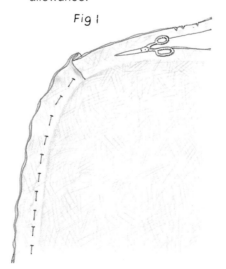

Fig I

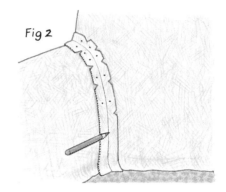

Fig 2

4 Fold the inside back fabric and repeat the process. From the point where the arm and back meet and right over the curve, make small marking tacks with coloured thread. Make a double stitch each side of the fold, along the fold line, at 2cm (¾ in) intervals. These will be your guide marks to make this seam, so make sure that these are very accurate. Trim the outside arm pieces to 2cm (¾ in) seam allowance and make notches. Also pencil along the seam line (fig 2).

5 Place the seat piece on to the chair. Join the front seat and arm in the same way. Pin the front gusset on and join to these two pieces. Again, make marking tacks along folded seam lines and, most importantly, at each point that three fabrics will need to meet - use a contrasting thread to save confusion. Pin the tuck-in allowances together and trim as necessary. Trim all seams. Check that each is notched (fig 3).

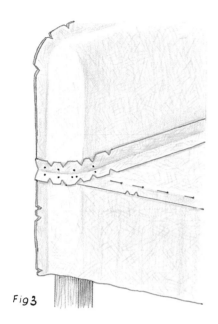

Fig 3

7 Slip the cover back on to make sure that it fits perfectly. Finger-fold each seam so that it faces the same direction through its length. Pull the fabric tight over the arms and back corners, pin the backs and arms together and push in the tuck in. Mark any adjustments with tacks.

Measure from the floor 25cm (10 in) all around and mark with pins. Remove chair cover and cut fabric away along this line. Stitch piping along this line 1.5cm (⅝ in) from the edge.

8 You will need to decide the length you wish your chair skirt to be – see variations on next page. We chose a short skirt, finished length 12cm (5 in). Cut a piece of main fabric and a piece of lining 5cm (2 in) deeper than the finished skirt size and 4cm (1 ½ in) longer than the piped line.

Cut a piece of strong paper to the size of the skirt to make the scalloped template. Mark the paper into sections for the sides, front and back lengths. Draw around a wine glass or saucer to make scallops which fit exactly between each section. The same scallop size may not fit each side – keep the depth the same but adjust the width of the scallops to fit.

Pin the template to the main fabric and, leaving 1.5cm (⅔ in) seam allowance, cut around the pattern carefully (fig 4a).

6 Cut out your fabric pieces following the pattern exactly and mark with small tags pinned to the right side of each. If you are using a plain fabric this step is essential to avoid making two left arms by mistake. Transfer all notches and marking tacks. Spend as much time as you need for the pattern to be accurate - if this process is short-cut the cover will not fit and you will spend more time re-doing seams.

Pipe all around the outside arm and the outside back. Make the top corner darts. Pin the inside arm to the outside back and stitch together from 10cm (4 in) above the top of each arm. Pin the inside arms to the outside arms and stitch between the back and seat joins. Join the inside back to both arms, matching tacks exactly along the curve. Join the seat and skirt pieces in the same way.

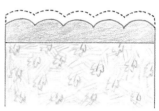

Fig 4a

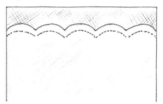

Fig 4b

Pin the lining to the fabric front and stitch around the scallops 1.5cm (⅔ in) from the raw edges (fig 4b). Trim away excess fabric, snipping tight into the points. Turn to the right side and press. Fold raw edge of lining under and slip stitch on the main cover, below piping.

9 Cut two strips of fabric 1, each 10cm (4 in) wide and the length of the back opening plus 4cm (1 ½ in). Stitch each to the main fabric using the 2cm (¾ in) seam allowance.

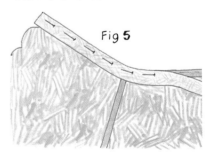

Fig 5

Press the seams and raw edges under 1.5cm (⅝ in). Fold in half, slip stitch to the stitching line and neaten ends. Stitch poppers or ties to close. Neaten seams and press.

Project 6: *Making Sofa and Chair Covers*

Skirt Variations

- Add a frill or box-pleated short skirt to the measured line

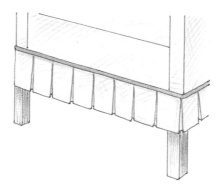

- Make a full length skirt

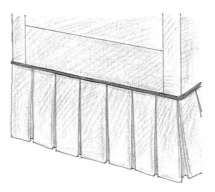

- Use both fabrics to make a pennanted skirt

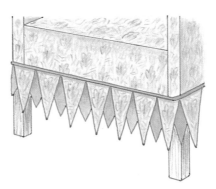

Arm Variations

Scroll: Cut fabric pieces for the front of the arms. Pin in place and pin the outside and the inside arms to it, following the shape.

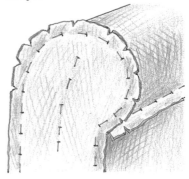

Club: Cut the arm piece to fit along the whole arm and pin the inside and outside arms to it carefully.

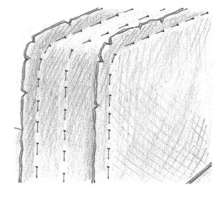

OTHER OPTIONS

Florals, formal stripes and a delicious woven fabric featuring snowflake patterns – these are just a few of the fabrics suitable for upholstery.

Blue and white stripes are a firm favourite for upholstery with many people. Here, floral and patterned cushions give the chair a more informal look. The centre cushion is made of the same fabric as the full curtains just seen to the left of the chair.

45

Project 7:
· · · · · · · · · · ·

Covers for Kitchen Chairs

E very country in the world has its own traditional design of kitchen chair, with some cultures preferring the wood left simply waxed to show its natural beauty and others favouring a painted look. Seats are generally made of wood, rush or cane and, whilst these simple chairs are ideally suited to the kitchens for which they were designed, being small but very sturdy, the seats are not upholstered and therefore often not very comfortable. Making a simple seat cushion (squab) extends the use of kitchen chairs and allows them to be dressed up or down.

Squab cushions must be attached to the legs of chairs to prevent them falling off when used. Ties, cords, laces, elasticated bands and buttoned tabs are all practical options. Make short or long ties and tie in a bow, or bind them around the chair leg for a tight fit. Remember, ties must always be sewn in very securely as they do sustain a good deal of wear and friction.

Seat cushions should ideally to be washable so that spills may be immediately dealt with and, if you make them reversible, they can lead a double life. Choose a hardwearing fabric, patterned so that small spots do not show easily.

Materials

- fabric 1 - 48 x 41cm (19 ¼ x 16 ⅜ in)
  41 x 16cm (16 ⅜ x 6 ¾ in) approx.
  137 x 20cm (55 x 8 in) approx.
- fabric 2 - 48 x 41cm (19 ¼ x 16 ⅜ in)
  41 x 16cm (16 ⅜ x 6 ¾ in) approx.
  137 x 20cm (55 x 8 in) approx.
- piping cord to go around twice - 4m (4 ½ yd)
- 2 laces, each 1m (40 in) long
- 5mm (¼ in) stationery riveting set
  or fabric for ties, 45 x 24cm (18 x 9 ½ in)
- 2cm (¾ in) foam or feather pad

Chair Cover
Our chair measured approximately 45 x 38cm (18 x 15 ¼ in) and we have made the cover reversible.

Make a template of your chair seat, using brown paper or newspaper cut just slightly larger than the seat. Tape the paper to all four sides and, with a thick crayon, draw on to the

paper following the edge of the seat. To get close to the seat back leg cut outs, tear the paper a little so that it lies flat enough for you to draw an accurate shape.

Bright colour plays an important role in both the painted chair frame and the fabric covering the chair seat. If using one strong colour for the paintwork, also use strong colours in the fabric, otherwise one will dominate the other. The same rule applies should you decide to use pale colours.

OTHER OPTIONS

A combination of floral and geometric patterns, plus green and orange, is unusual but effective. Try this scheme or mix and match your own colourways, but use the same theme.

Kitchen chairs can be dressed up brilliantly. For an informal room you do not need to have a matching set, as these odd chairs (which were collected separately and each painted a bright colour) illustrate. Pretty loose covers with a spring motif dress the chairs for a party. The valances have been left short to emphasize the informality of both the furnishings and the room.

Project 8:
. . . .

Covering Dining Chairs

Lightly-fitting furniture covers, known as slip covers, can be made for most types of furniture and may be used purely for their decorative appearance or to cover a less than lovely underneath - perhaps a seat needs re-upholstering or the wood needs to be stripped and re-polished?

Wood, cane and partly-upholstered side chairs are particularly good choices for treatment in this manner and will respond to all sorts of designs and styles of fabric - small and large checks, on their own or mixed together, dimity prints for a child's bedroom or nursery, plain colours with complementary piping and ties - let your imagination run wild. Chosen carefully, a very strong, colourful, dramatic pattern could sit well on a set of dining chairs in an all-white room.

C h a i r   C o v e r
You will need to measure your chair to plan the pieces and to estimate the amount of fabric which you will need:

inside back	A x B
outside back	C x D
seat	E x F
gusset	G x H
skirt	J

Materials

- white cotton or linen as estimated (see above)
- self-piping to fit around both sides of gusset and chair back (see page 62)
- 4 self-ties - 60 x 12mm (24 x ½ in) rouleaux (see page 00)

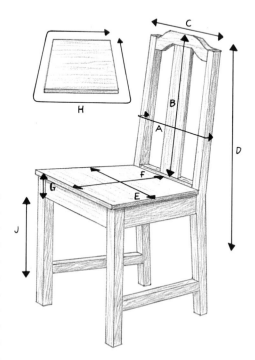

1 Cut out your pieces as measured, adding 6cm (2¾ in) seam allowance to each measurement and allowing 1.5 times fullness for the skirt. Mark the centre backs of chair and finger-fold the fabric in half lengthways.

2 Pin to the chair front and back. If the chair has a completely wooden frame you will need to wind some tape tightly around to give a base for pinning. Pin the front to the back against the frame. This cover will be very loose but the finished shape will still need to follow the line of the chair. Ease any fullness, pleating or gathering corners as necessary.

This elegant dining chair has been covered with a pure white cotton loose cover. The deep frill is an added decorative element, creating a simple, elegant style at a reasonable cost. The self-piping adds the finishing touch. The cover can be drycleaned and will last for as long as you want to have this look in your dining room.

Project 8: *Covers for Dining Chairs*
• • • • • • • • •

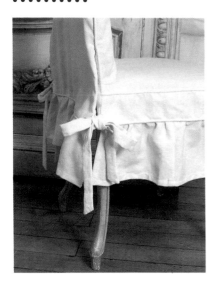

3 When you are happy with the cover, move the pins to make the cover baggy but still a good shape at the top. Trim seam allowance to 2cm (¾ in) and notch. Pin the seat piece to the chair. Pin the gusset to the seat following the line of the chair seat exactly. Trim seams to 2cm (¾ in) and notch.

4 Stitch the piping cord around sides and top of right side of the outside back. Stitch the back to the front, from 15cm (6 in) above the chair seat on each side. Stitch the chair seat back to the inside back. Stitch piping around the rest of the chair seat. Cut the gusset down to 8cm (3 ¼ in) and stitch piping to the lower side, leaving 2cm (¾ in) seam allowance. Pin the other side to the chair seat, snipping where necessary for fabric to lie flat. Stitch, neaten seams and press.

5 Put chair cover back on. Pin back to front at seat level and mark tie positions with coloured tacks. Measure from the floor upwards and cut off the excess fabric at the back to line up with bottom of the gusset. Make up ties as shown on page 22.

6 Make two skirts: one to fit across the back and one to fit around the front. Make a 1.5cm (⅝ in) double turning on sides and hem. Run a gathering thread 1.5cm (⅝ in) from the top. Gather

up evenly and pin along the back, between the side seam allowance and along the gusset, leaving the seam allowance at each end. Stitch, neaten seams and press.

7 Cut two strips of fabric 6cm (2 ⅜ in) wide, each twice the length of the openings plus 4cm (1½ in). Pin one tie to each of the marked points. Pin one strip to each side, right sides together and stitch. Press, fold over to enclose raw edges, neaten ends and slip stitch to the first stitching line. Press, arrange the cover on chair and tie the ties.

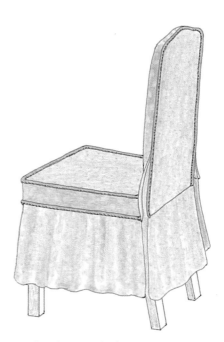

Marking the position for the ties.

Try cool blue in a pattern or stripe, rather than our monotone chair cover. Any of these patterns would make an interesting cover, particularly if the room's background scheme was cream or white, and the chairs had chrome legs.

Ladder-backed country dining chairs usually have caned or wooden seats and are known more for their lovely shapes than for comfort. A thin padded seat adds comfort and the straight skirt adds a tailored look which is not 'dressy' for these chairs. Long ties can be wound around the legs several times to keep the cover in place.

Project 9:
. . . .

Dressing Up Garden Chairs

Garden chairs are often well designed and comfortable, with the additional benefits that they are relatively inexpensive to buy and can be dressed in fabric covers for an almost infinite variety of uses. Why not make several sets of covers for your chairs: one set for casual use in the garden, another for elegant summer supper parties and yet another set of covers for indoor use during the winter months - perhaps as extra side chairs in bedrooms or bathrooms. For additional seating, bring your chairs in from the terrace to help out in the dining room. One set of chairs and two sets of covers can be very useful for a move into a first flat with a limited budget.

Even if you have no garden, an outdoor chair covered with a simple fabric can be transformed into a bedside 'table', or a bedroom or bathroom chair. Make simple covers to use in the kitchen for breakfast.

Chair Cover
Measure your chair and plan how to best cut the fabric, following the illustration.

outside back height and width	A
inside back height and width	B
seat width and depth	C
front height and width	D
side height at front and	
back and width	E

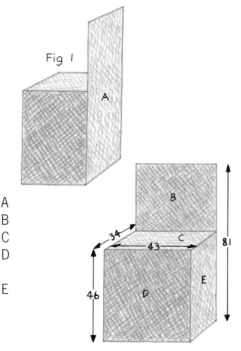

Fig 1

Our chair was 81cm (32 ⅜ in) high from the top of the back, with a seat size of 43 x 34cm (17 ¼ x 13 ½ in) and 46cm (18 ⅜ in) from the floor. We allowed a 3cm (1 ¼ in) seam allowance to all pieces.

Materials

- fabric as planned (see above)
- 8 ties, each 50 x 2cm (20 x ¾ in)
- 4 ties, each 15cm x 12 mm (6 x 1½ in)
- polyester wadding and a piece of lining to quilt the seat (optional)

1 Cut out all pieces with the inside and outside backs as one piece. Make a 1.5cm (⅝ in) seam on the sides and hems of all pieces except the seat. With right sides together, join the back piece to the back of the seat piece using the 3cm (1 ¼ in) seam allowance. Cut back to 1.5cm (⅝ in) and neaten. Join the two sides and the front in the same way with seam allowances of 3cm (1 ¼ in) cut back to 1.5cm (⅝ in) and neatened.

Take a peak under this smart but casual cover and you would be surprised at how ordinary it is. Yet a simple cover turns it into a desirable item.

Project 9: *Dressing up Garden Chairs*
• • • • • • • • • •

3 Stitch the short ties opposite each other to the seam where the back and seat join, approximately 6cm (2 ⅜ in) in from either side. Press cover and arrange over the chair. Tie the two short ties to the chair frame to prevent the cover moving forwards in use. Tie the other ties.

Other options

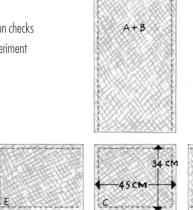
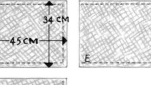

Hard-wearing blue and cream pure cotton checks are also suitable for a casual cover. Experiment with colour combinations.

2 Stitch the long ties to the back and seat as shown, and approximately 8cm (3 ¼ in) below the seat on the two front panels.

Variation

You might prefer to quilt the seat following the instructions for the Deck Chair (see pages 57-58). If so, make up the cover completely, lay wadding over the seat section, tack and stitch. Cut a piece of lining fabric to the seat size plus seam allowances, press under seam allowances and stitch all around, encasing the wadding plus all the seams

Quilting Pattern

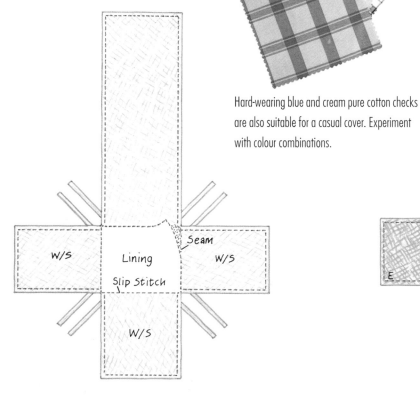

Project 10:
• • • • • • • • • •

Deck Chairs

Deck chairs are designed for use in the garden, on the patio, round the pool or on the beach. Deck chairs are designed to be cheap and functional and come with a basic cover, usually a simple design, brightly coloured and weatherproof, tacked to the frame at the top and bottom. To personalise your deck chair, it is easy to remove this cover and make your own. Choose a fabric which is very strong, printed in colours which will not fade on the first sunny day and which will work well with your other garden chair covers. Your cover choice is unlikely to be waterproof, so remember to bring the chair in at the first sign of rain; a washable fabric will not be damaged but will need drying time.

Another style of deck chair is now commonly called a 'director's' chair; these have a straighter seat position, a sturdier frame with arms, and they fold up side to side. Director's chairs can also be re-covered in any strong woven fabric by copying the original pieces - or make a padded cover following these instructions and tie to the seat and back, over the existing cover.

Chair Cover
Our cover measured 105 x 50cm (42 x 20 in) and we used the same fabric for back and front.

Firstly, measure the original cover from just under the top rail to just before the bottom rail. This will be the finished measurement of your cover. Remove the old cover and paint the wood with a weatherproof paint.

Materials

- fabric 1 - 105 x 50cm (42 x 20 in)
  50 x 40cm (20 x 16 in)
- fabric 2 - 105 x 50cm (42 x 20 in)
  50 x 40cm (920 x 16 in)
- 2 pieces of 4 oz polyester wadding, each 105 x 50cm (42 x 20 in)
- 4cm (1 ½ in) binding or ribbed ribbon - 1 piece, 3m (3½ yd)
  12 pieces, 15cm (6 in)
- 12 button press stud kit

1 Place fabric 2 on your worktable, right side down. Place the two layers of wadding over and then fabric 1, right side up. Pin all around and through the centre width and length. Tack the whole piece in 16cm (6 ⅜ in) squares. If, like us, you choose a squared design, you should follow the printed pattern.

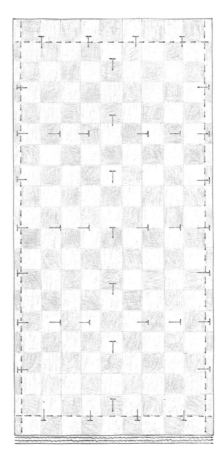

Project 10: *Deck Chairs*
• • • • • • • • • •

2 When the whole is firmly tacked together, machine along the squared lines. Always start from the top and work towards the bottom. Start from the same side at all times, so if the fabric does move slightly it will move in the same direction and will not show ugly ruckles. Unpick the tacking. Pin the short strips of tapes to the top and bottom against fabric 2 as shown. Stitch in place.

3 Mark with pins 2cm (¾ in) inside the raw edges all around and make a light pencil mark to join pins. Place the binding tape against these lines, covering the raw edges, and pin. At each corner fold under to make a mitre. Pin securely. Machine stitch all around close to binding edge.

4 Fold the binding tape over to the back. Pin and slip stitch down. Fit the cover on the deck chair and pin the tabs in place. Mark the press stud position and make fastening according to the instructions with the kit.

5 To make the foot rest, follow the instructions for the main cover and stitch the tabs so that they fit in between the main cover tabs, as shown.

Other options

Bold squares of colour in deeper tones make a smart alternative combination. Ensure the fabric you choose is waterproof.

Give an old director's chair a burst of new life with a new cover. To make, measure its old cover, add seam allowances and sew. Use a waterproof, hard-wearing natural fabric.

Strong stripes are traditional for deck chairs and this one could be quilted and bound with a strong contrast for an individual look.

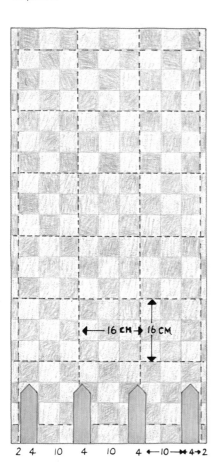

16 CM ⟷ 16 CM

2   4   10   4   10   4 ◀—10—▶ 4 ▶ 2

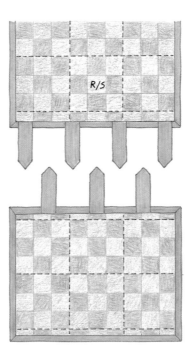

R/S

Section three
Stitches and Seams

You do not have to be an expert needle person to make cushions and covers; you just need to acquire a few basic sewing skills. Descriptions of the stitches most commonly used are given below, along with instructions for the seams you will be using.

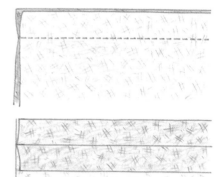

Buttonhole Stitch

This stitch is not only used to make buttonholes but in any situation which requires extra strength. The thread is twisted at the front of the stitch allowing it to resist abrasion against metal poppers, hooks and eyes, brass rings, and so on. This stitch can be worked to cover a raw edge or over a folded edge.

Working from left to right, push the needle up through the fabric pointing away from the edge. Twist the thread around the point and pull the needle through. Keep the threads as straight as possible and pull so that a knot forms on the edge of the fabric.

Slip Stitch

Work from right to left with a single thread. Fasten the thread with two small stitches hidden inside the seam. Bring the needle out through the top of the folded edge, pick up two threads of fabric then work through the fold of the fabric. Slide the needle along then come out of the fold to make the next stitch.

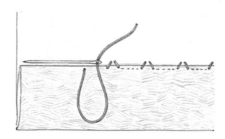

French Seam

This seam encloses the raw edges of fabric and is used when an untidy edge might be visible. Pin wrong sides of fabric together and stitch approximately 6mm (¼ in) from the raw edges. Refold with right sides together, pin and stitch again just beyond the first stitching line, to enclose the edges. When stitching heavier fabrics, allow 12mm (½ in) for the first stitching line.

Flat Seam

With right sides pinned together, machine stitch inside the raw edge; most covers require a 1.5cm (⅝ in) seam allowance, but for loose covers use 2cm (¾ in). Remove pins and press seam allowance flat from the back. Turn over and press from the front over a cloth.

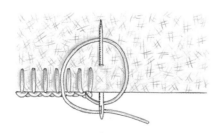

Inserting a Zip

If your zip is to be placed in a simple gusset: Open up the zip fully. Press under 2.5cm (1 in) of both pieces of fabric, the length of the zip. Pin one side close to the zip and stitch as close to the teeth as possible.

Close up the zip and place the fold over the zip so that the previous stitching line is not visible. Pin about 1.5cm (⅝ in) from the fold and at right angles, pinning the fold down. Stitch along the pin line.

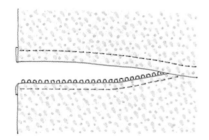

If your zip is to go in a cushion with piping: stitch the back and fronts together for approximately 4cm (1 ½ in) from each end. Press the non-piped side under to the seam allowance. Open up the zip fully. Pin to the piping as closely

as possible with the teeth against the piping cord and stitch.

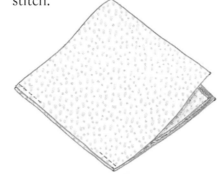

Black and white cherubs feature here. There is a zip along the back of the seat cover; and each small round cushion has a zip at the back, too.

Lie the cushion flat and close the zip. From the front, pin the folded piece over the zip covering all teeth. Pin at right angles and stitch as close to the teeth as possible. When almost at the end, lift the machine foot and open the zip so that the slider is out of the way

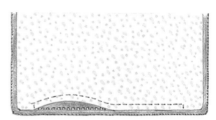

Piping

Piping may be cut on the straight or on the cross. The general rule is, if piping is to be used in straight lines, it will be easier to handle straight: if it is to be bent around corners, it should be cut on the cross. To make 3mm (⅛ in) piping cord, cut 6cm (2 ⅜ in) wide strips. All joins should be made on the cross to minimise bulk when folded and the ends should be cut across at an angle of 90 degrees.

To Cut on the Cross

With the fabric flat on the table, fold one bottom corner as if making a 30cm (12 in) square. Cut along the fold line. Mark pencil lines from this cut edge 6cm (2 ½ in) from each other; cut along these lines. Hold two pieces together as if making a continuous strip, flip the top one over and hold. Stitch together where the two fabrics cross.

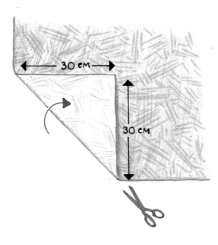

To Cut on the Straight

Cut lengths as long as possible and hold two strips together as if making a continuous length. Trim away both corners at an angle of 45 degrees, hold together and flip the top one over. Stitch together where the two pieces cross.

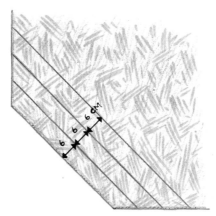

To Make Up Piping

Press seams flat and cut away excess corners. Fold in half along the length and insert the piping cord. Machine stitch to encase, approximately 3mm (⅛ in) from the cord.

Pinning Piping On

Always pin piping so that the raw edges of piping exactly line up with the raw edges of the main fabric. The seam allowance is usually 1.5cm (⅝ in). Begin work at the bottom of the cushion and, at each corner, stop 1.5cm (⅝ in) from the end and snip right into the piping stitching line. Fold the piping sharply and pin to make a square corner.

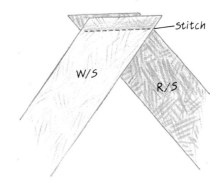

Pin along the stitching line and also at right angles, especially near the corners. These right-angled pins can be left in whilst machining and will keep the piping flat.

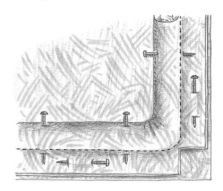

When pinning around curves, the piping cord should be snipped at approximately l.5cm (⅝ in) intervals to enable it to remain flat around a convex curve. You will need to cut notches at similar intervals for a concave curve.

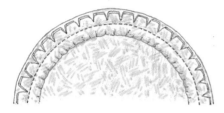

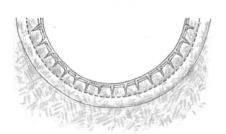

Joining Piping

When you return to the start, cut the piping off leaving an overlap of 6cm (2 ¼ in). Unpick the casing and cut away the cord so that the two ends butt up. Fold the piping fabric across at an angle of 45 degrees and cut along this fold. Fold under 12mm (½ in) and pin securely before stitching.

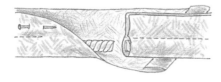

Plaids and tartans are always popular for scatter cushions and need no more decoration than matching cords and tassels to look inviting. Here, the cushions have been piped with a thick cord, and finished with tassels at each corner. The tassels are a small detail, without which the cushion would not have quite the desired effect.

Index